On the Job

Dona Herweck Rice

Publishing Credits

Rachelle Cracchiolo, M.S.Ed., *Publisher*
Conni Medina, M.A.Ed., *Managing Editor*
Nika Fabienke, Ed.D., *Content Director*
Véronique Bos, *Creative Director*
Shaun N. Bernadou, *Art Director*
Carol Huey-Gatewood, M.A.Ed., *Editor*
John Leach, *Assistant Editor*
Courtney Roberson, *Senior Graphic Designer*

Image Credits: All images from iStock and/or Shutterstock.

Library of Congress Cataloging-in-Publication Data

Names: Rice, Dona, author.
Title: On the job / Dona Herweck Rice.
Description: Huntington Beach, CA : Teacher Created Materials, [2019] | Identifiers: LCCN 2018029729 (print) | LCCN 2018033698 (ebook) | ISBN 9781493899357 | ISBN 9781493898619
Subjects: LCSH: Readers (Primary)
Classification: LCC PE1119 (ebook) | LCC PE1119 .R466 2019 (print) | DDC 428.6/2--dc23
LC record available at https://lccn.loc.gov/2018029729

Teacher Created Materials
5301 Oceanus Drive
Huntington Beach, CA 92649-1030
www.tcmpub.com

ISBN 978-1-4938-9861-9

Printed in China
Nordica.082018.CA21800936

You can listen and look some time each day.

You can 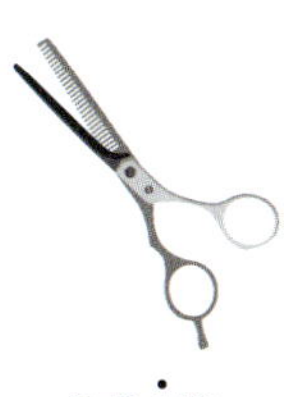 and 

snip comb

some time each day.

You can  cut and  mix

some time each day.

You can  read and  write

some time each day.

You can  and 

measure saw

some time each day.

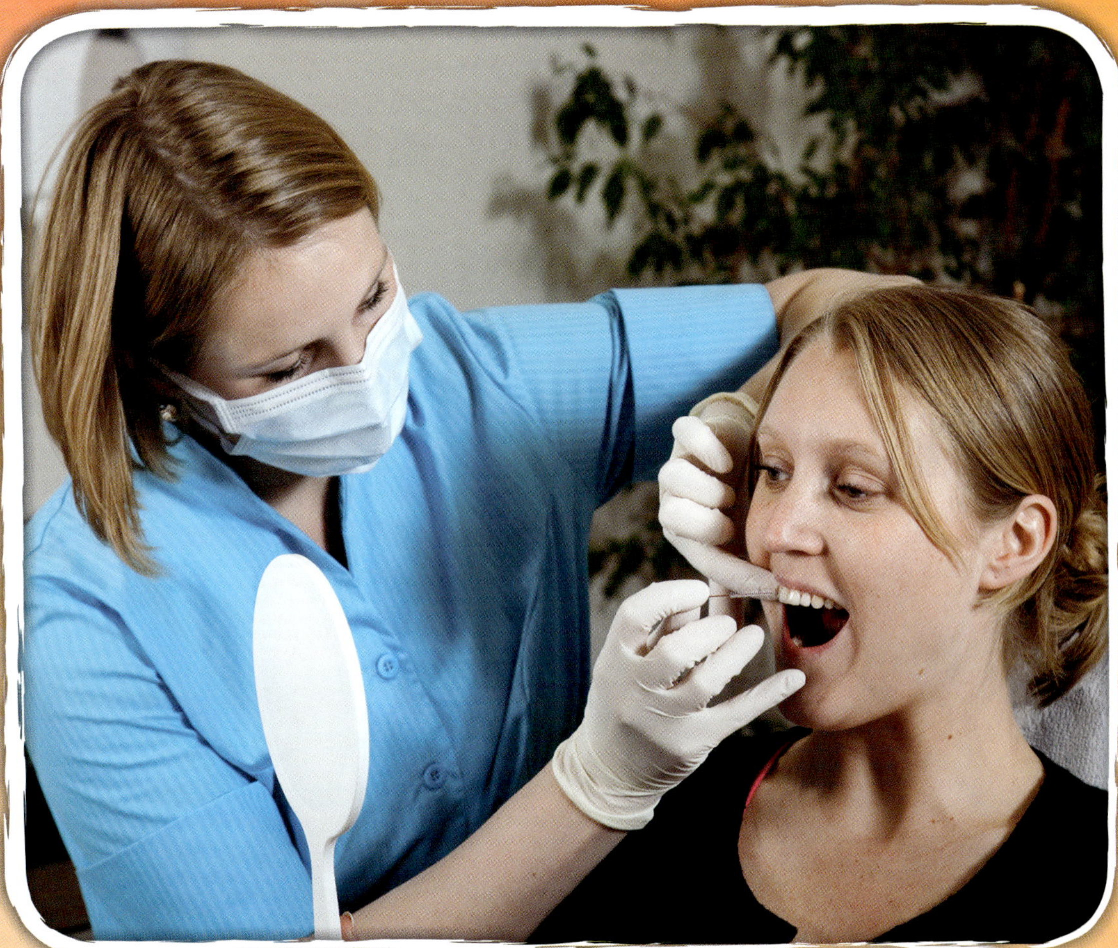

You can  brush and 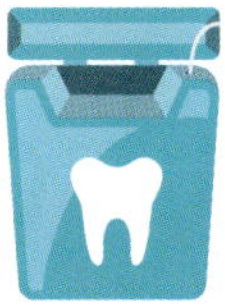 floss

some time each day.

You can  and 

plant drive

some time each day.

You can  water and  dig

some time each day.

You can 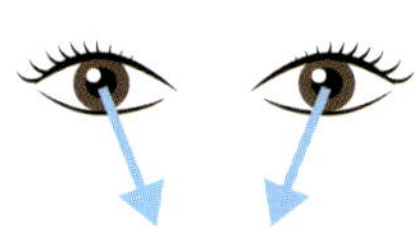 and 

look write

some time each day.

You can  and 

play sing

some time each day.

High-Frequency Words

New Words

can
day
each
some
time

Review Words

and
you